CW00487281

Baited

Tim Cranmore

Black Pear Press

Best Wishes

Tim Cranmore

Barred
Tim Cranmore

Copyright © 2014 Tim Cranmore
First published 2014 by **Black Pear Press Limited**
www.blackpear.net

A CIP catalogue record of this book is available from
the British Library

ISBN 978-1-910322-08-6

Design: Martin Driscoll
www.martindriscolldesign.com
Published in association with the Worcestershire
Literary Festival
www.worcslitfest.co.uk
Cover image: Colt Chaos Design

Being bard is not a comfort zone.
Being barred is also not a comfort zone.
Being a barred bard just gives rise to bad jokes, but
Being barred along with Pentonville, Beethoven's seventh
symphony, and the barred warbler,
Has its compensations…

About The Author

After starting life as a placental analyst, Tim Cranmore developed his career as the UK's only maker of baroque recorders. A logical step at the time but one which, in retrospect, totally defies all rational analysis. He now lives and works in Malvern.

Dedication

My thanks go out to the Worcestershire Literary
Festival [aka: the Worcs LitFest & Fringe] for
supporting me as their Third Bard.
At this moment in time I am about to be replaced, but
hey! - The Fourth Bard cometh.
I'm sure we will be friends.

Also available without prescription and by the same
author:
'Obedience Training For Recorders' published by
Peacock Press
http://www.recordermail.co.uk/acatalog/Books.html

Table Of Contents

I Water

Mermaid

1. Noye's Fludde

Old Noah felt a mighty prat,
He'd parked his ark on Ararat.
When God looked down he said, "My dear,
You really can't park that ark 'ere,"
But Noah said, "My God, don't fuss,
I've just invented Pets 'R' Us,
And as a deal twixt you and me,
I'll do you buy one, get one free,"
"Bogoff!" said God, "that's right" said Noah,
And throwing open wide the door,
The animals with a mighty roar,
Spread out to populate the earth,
And Noah thought, now what's it worth.
But when God opened Noah's bill,
He felt a little faint and ill,

1

And bellowed out, "Before me fall!
My Hellfire shall consume you all,"
But Noah said, "I have to dash,
In God we trust, the rest pay cash."

2. On My Bidet - For Catherine

It was Monday on my bidet, and I'm sitting by myself,
While a plastic pink Madonna, looks benignly from the shelf.

It was Tuesday on my bidet, and the kids are off to school,
And I tell them that I'm quite alright, that bidet sitting's cool.

It was Wednesday on my bidet, and my husband's quite uptight,
'Cos he hasn't had his supper, or his weekly conjugal rights.

It was Thursday on my bidet, and the doctor's been and gone,
He said I could use wet wipes, but I said I'd soldier on.

It was Friday on my bidet, and my circulation's dire,
But I've got a cosy blanket, and a small electric fire.

It was Saturday on my bidet, starting to hallucinate,
From the lack of food and water, and a deepening sense of fate,
When the plastic pink Madonna floated down and heaved a sigh,
Hovered out of reach, and fixed me with a purple sparkly eye,
And she told me "Jesus loves you, He was God's almighty son,
He can answer all your questions" and I said "I've got just one,
In the name of all that's holy, how d'you turn this bidet on?"

Now it's Sunday on my bidet, I'm a happy smiling

mum,
While the swift refreshing waters, flow delightfully up
my bum,
And I'm going down to breakfast, there's a space up on
the shelf,
And the plastic pink Madonna's in the bidet,
By herself.

3. The School Run

The River Severn, flowing deep and wide,
With tidal rushes, fragile muddy banks and swirling
curlicues,
Reflecting the cathedral's rugged side,
Kept all barbarians at bay.
The Welsh, the Herefordians,
The smelly folk who thought the Malvern Hills were
pretty cool,
Could never send their kids to school in Worcester,
But could only stare, or try their luck in leaky boats,
Commuting with a muttered prayer to heathen river
gods,
To make their daily journey free from care.

And then they built the bridge,
As fine an edifice as ever spanned a river's breadth,
Yet still a narrow way between two lands,
Choked with traffic of a horsey, sheepy kind,
That made the school run perilous and slow for Mrs
Smith and little Jo.
But others followed thick and fast,
At Holt Heath, Upton, Tewkesbury,
A flashy new by-pass, and finally the motorway,
Triumphantly proclaiming that the other side of Severn
stream
Need not remain a distant dream,
For students, tradesmen, wage slaves,
Mums whose husbands worked in grimy Brum,
But raised their kids in groomed and thatched, half-
timbered bliss,
Fed with organic greens from Sainsbury's,
Praying that sky high prices for their homes
Would keep away the great unwashed
As surely as the Severn stream once kept away the
Welsh, the Herefordians,
From Worcester's academic dream.

But Mr Smith sat in his car and fumed,
As all the bridges in the world
Could never make the journey home at 6pm.
Go faster than when medieval man
Could only queue to cross the single, sheep-clogged
span
That linked those Severn banks in days gone by.

"New roads make traffic" so the mantra runs,
So when the planners say they mean
To run a six-lane motorway to Aberystwyth,
Arise all rank Malvernians,
Destroy the bridges, mine the by-pass,
Stand on Severn's muddy brink,
And tell them what you really think
And raise the shout, "Keep out! Keep out!"
You used to cross on every whim,
But now you'll have to bloody swim!

4. Tsunami

Before the wave without an end,
You ran, you had no plan, except
Perhaps to get to higher ground,
So that the debris-stricken wave,
Would flow around and join again, to leave you on an island of
your thoughts, without the pain.
And on the foaming crest of
The wave without an end jostled happily,
A brightly painted silver, shiny Honda, a Toyota Prius, a Nissan,
That looked as though they still belonged,
In rush hour Tokyo, as they rushed on driverless into
happy suburbs that themselves were floating freely,
On the wave without an end.
Each of them was made,
by a man who had a plan.
Each lovingly created part, a wonder of industrial art,
That now began to rot in salty water's grip,
Because the man who made the plan,
Had never thought to help them float, like a boat, or a ship.
Like your ideas, flashing, shining,
Lovingly created, on a wave without an end, jostling brightly,
For attention.
Do you feel you want to run
To higher ground, and let them float,
Around the hill on which you sit, alone?
The mist inside my eye joins the mist before my face,
The wave inside your head meets the wave behind your back.
We can neither see nor think.

5. Cause

I lie on mud and watch the gentle flow.
A tattered fragment idly floating by.
Says 'Sainsbury's' and I don't know why.
I love this silty Severn stream,
And what it bears along,
And when it clears I see above,
A faded, dappled sun,
And I remember looking down
To view my present bed,
That hot sun on my back.
Before I fell.
Before the sword cut deep.
Before my sight turned red,
And ask, does the cathedral that I briefly glimpsed
reflected there still rise above the bank, or did it fall like
me in time's slow motion dance?
The boys that used to swim above my head have long
since gone,
but shadowy hands still throw white bread to whiter
swans,
A whiteness only kings could taste,
When I still lived.
And now I rest, and drift, and dream,
My Royalist cause must surely have prevailed.
To make it worth my time, my life, my sword, my
death,
my family's loss...
My long sleep.
A tattered fragment idly floating by.
Says Tesco.
And I really don't know why.

6. The Mermaid And The Mason

Almost one thousand years ago,
On River Severn's eastern side,
St Wulfstan planned the world to show,
His great cathedral, Worcester's pride.

And so from all across the shires,
The carpenters and masons came,
To carve the stone in rich designs,
To glorify God's gracious name.

The Bishop kept a watchful eye,
As stone was carved with beauty rare,
And Tom, the master mason's son,
Made angels dance and demons glare.

St Wulfstan pledged him by his hand,
As his reward, and his alone,
To carve his likeness, there to stand
High above the Bishop's throne.

That Spring it rained, a dreadful time.
The River Severn swelled and grew,
As water from a thousand streams
Fed its appetite anew.

Young Tom, one dark and stormy night,
Was walking back to hearth and home,
He paused in moonshine's fitful light,
And looked upon the flood below.

Against the famous Worcester bridge,
The debris of the thousand streams,
Rose and fell in gulf and ridge,
While whirlpools danced with spouts and steams.

And then with livid lightning flash,
He saw her in the arch's shade,

Thorny brambles held her fast,
Tangled roots a prison made.

Her shining tail was torn and bruised.
About her face, her golden hair
Was tangled like a Gordian knot,
With rain-lashed willow branches there.

The lamprey sucked against her breast,
And crayfish gnawed her fingers neat,
And leeches gorged with silver blood
Surged with the flow, and fell replete.

Without a thought, without a care,
Tom dived into the depths below.
He cut her hair, her golden hair,
The willow branches let her go.

But parting with a tortured scream,
The dam was burst, the arch released
The pent up wrath of Severn stream.
A thousand valleys fed the beast.

With grinding, cold, remorseless speed,
The tumbling forests bore them down,
Far from help, in dreadful need,
Tom prayed as he prepared to drown,
But mermaids have the strength of ten,
She fought the willow, fir and ash,
And in her arms she took him then,
Beneath the flood's torrential dash.

And with his mouth embraced in hers,
She led him through the waters brown,
And on a bed of softest silt,
With tender touch she laid him down.

Above their heads the river boiled,

But there they loved and there they lay.
He breathed her life, she gave her all,
Until the breaking of the day.

The pike and salmon turned their backs,
The watercress gave dappled shade,
Dragonflies patrolled the banks,
And billowing eels a curtain made.
Water beetles clicked their heels,
Skaters danced a measure neat,
The damselfly in homage kneeled,
And water nymphs brought snails to eat.

With one last breath she filled his soul,
From her he fed, from her he drank,
Then lifting him with loving care
She laid him on the eastern bank.

And so they found him, pale and cold,
But with a fire that burned inside,
And in his eyes her image gold,
Who saved his life from that dark tide.

For thirty years Tom marked his place,
But in the night he worked alone,
'Til, where he'd carved his youthful face,
Another stood beside his own.

And if you look so very high,
Way above the Bishop's throne,
Where incense wafts and music sighs,
Choirs sing and priests intone.

Above the nave, where arches rise.
A mermaid carved in yellow stone,
Looks with limpid, timeless eyes,
For him to see, and him alone.

II Growing Old

Aged One

1. Ball Games

In my sporting schooldays,
The rules for self preservation
Went like this.
If a ball landed at your feet
Run...
If a ball landed in your arms,
Throw it away...
If a ball landed on your head,
Play dead...
If the ball was over there,
Hide here...
If the ball was over here,
Hide there...
If you needed to kick, catch,
If you needed to catch, kick.
I soon realised that disqualification was safer
Than participation.

2. High Street

In Glastonbury town,
Not every few shops, not every other shop,
But each and every shop,
Has a pixie in the window, a mushroom, a bright-eyed resin faerie,
Crystals shining UV blue, dragons hatched from raku eggs.
Packs of tarot cards, self-help, self-healing,
'Try Tantric sex and meet your inner Goddess' books,
Passed endlessly from one lost hippy to another.
Hand drawn, grubby postcards pinned ten deep on every health food notice board,
"I can heal you, help you, energize you, crystallize you,
Balance your chakras, fight your inner demons,
Explain your dreams, pry and poke and prod and penetrate."
Each and every yoga discipline with Guna, Prana, Star and Spiral,
Names their mothers' never used in 1952.
No wonder Tesco fled to Street just up the road!
And as the sun warms benches, and the first guitarist
Slouches, blinking from a dark vinyl-filled den,
The first faint whiff of skunk wafts lazily past the rows of Indian frocks,
And soon the street, Glastonbury High Street, is, indeed,
High...

3. The Death Of A Friend

How did the finger miss me that took my friend away?
What was the margin, inches, miles?
Did it miss because I smiled and moved across the bar
to talk to someone else?
Is it blind or does it have a cosmic GPS that led to him
and not to me?
I wonder if it cuts its nail, or bites it to the quick before
It gets on with the job?
Or if I see it coming, will its nail be long and grimy?
If I duck to tie my shoelace will it take the one behind
me?

Fate's finger, you have a lot to answer for.
Abandoned children, grieving widows, sickened folk
who search the rubble with their own fingers bleeding,
sore.

My friend didn't see you there,
Perhaps a movement of the air he couldn't quite
describe, before he felt the pain, the nervelessness,
The loss of speech or thought, the panic, breathless,
strange.
Well let me warn you, fickle-fingered fate, you come for
me I'll...
What?
All I know is, somewhere in a cosmic file marked 'Tim',
the tale comes to an end.
And perhaps I'll see my friend.

4. One For The Over Fifties

When you're coming to the autumn of your life,
And you've waved goodbye to mortgage, kids and wife,
And the number of your days is worryingly small,
You look into the mirror, and the mirror says it all.

Your jowls are like the dewlaps of a bloodhound,
Your lines are like the canyons of Mars.
Your eyes are like two onions poached in ketchup,
From a lifetime spent 'til 2am in bars.
Your thinning hair is grey as mist in winter,
And your intellect is drowning in the ooze,
And your memory is a shadow of the one you used to
know,
Before you overdid the ciggies and the booze.

Your ears have lost their sense in both directions,
Though mosquitoes never bother you at all.
In the shower you can hardly see your kneecaps,
As your beer gut fills the space from wall to wall.
Your teeth are like a row of rotten tombstones,
And your nose is sprouting hair like summer grass,
And your sex appeal is drooping like a withered pink
balloon,
And your memory of love is fading fast

You thought you could attract a younger model,
That your maturity could beat the best of youth.
Just flash your credit cards and wear Armani,
And when she asks your age, don't tell the truth.
So with corsets, contacts, cocaine and Viagra,
You could party through the night and never stop,
But like the man whose barrel shot Niagara,
You're going to hit rock bottom when you stop.

When you're coming to the winter of your life,
And you've waved goodbye to mortgage, kids and wife,

And the number of your days is vanishingly small,
You look into the mirror, and the mirror said...
You horny old devil, you sexy old brute,
You can still strut your stuff, and your butt's kinda cute,
You're on the way up, so Botox that frown,
Grab the keys to the Ferrari, let's go out on the town!

5. Life

When our first cat, who had cancer, died, I cried.
I was surprised, and so would he have been because,
Although I took him to the vet, as yet we weren't the
best of friends,
Yet that was when he died, and that was when I cried.

Our second cat was not a fan
Of anyone that was a man, and
Ran away to hide, perhaps she'd
Had some tricky early days, with roughshod men with
violent ways,
So when I took her to the vet, as yet we weren't the
best of friends,
And that was when she died, and once again I cried.

I didn't cry, when my dad died.

III FOOD And Other Root Vegetables

My relationship to the carrot is purely musical. As a cylindrical, homogenous item approximately 15cm long, it is, of course, ideal material for making sopranino recorders.
The only advantage of using a tree is that it lasts longer.
However, for short term gratification, the carrot wins hands down.

1. Orange

There is nothing quite so orange as a carrot.
Not even easyJet is quite as bright.
And though orange peel is so,
It's a superficial show,
As the other side is messy stringy white.
Now not only is a carrot's skin so orange,
It's a truly feisty orange through and through.
It's orange on its top, and the orange never stops,
And a carrot's orange bottom's orange too.
The Orange Order isn't even orange!
William of Orange was a total fraud.
And the only person ever,
To get near that magic colour,
Owned a tanning lounge in Essex, name of Maud.
There's nothing quite so spiritual as a carrot,
And a Buddhist's robes are carrot-coloured too.
And in fact the Dalai Lama,
Was a secret carrot farmer,
And embraced his inner carrot through and through.
There is nothing quite as sexy as a carrot.
It never suffers from erectile doubt,
But gives erogenous delight,
Morning, noon and night,
And never shows a sign of wearing out.
Now when I die please bury me in orange.
In my carrot-coloured suit I'll feel so brave.
Oh, let me please go off in,
A carrot-coloured coffin,
With carrots planted all around my grave.
Give praise to the Almighty for the carrot.
Its qualities too great to number crunch
It's dramatic. It's ecstatic,
There's no root so charismatic,
It's my Shakespeare it's my bible, it's my lunch.

2. Psycho

I love a bag of scratchings
With a pint of English ale.
Every bit of little piggy,
From his schnozzle to his tail.
And the variety of shapes,
The knots and turns and twists,
Make them far more entertaining
Than a bag of nuts, or crisps.
There's the rather tasty fatty ones,
That melt in pools of lard,
And the ones that break your teeth,
'Cos they're really rather hard!
There's those little hairy stubbly bits
That irritate your colon,
And sometimes they say Danish,
Just 'cos that's where they come from.
And sometimes you may recognise a nipple or a bum,
But nothing quite prepared me
When I found one that said 'Mum'!

Now pigs are not well known to be
Tattooed from end to end,
To celebrate their parents,
Or a lady piggy friend,
So even Sherlock Holmes
Would reach the logical position
That my bag of porky scratchings
Held a sinister addition.
A family loving youngster,
Who lost his bright young life
In a squalid grease-smeared kitchen,
To a madman's flaying knife.
Some predatory psycho with
Ideas of playing God.
A new born Jack the Ripper,
Or a modern Sweeny Todd.

But I left it on my beer mat thinking,
Might not be so bad,
'Til I rummaged through the bag,
and found a scratching that said 'Dad'...
I ran out of the pub,
And threw the packet in the air,
And Mum and Dad and Gran and Sis,
Went flying everywhere.
In every bush and shadow,
I seemed to see a knife,
And I slammed the door and
Nailed it shut and trembled for my life.
I've gone off porky scratchings,
I'm vegetarian now.
My teeth will last me longer, my
Cholesterol's gone down
But I know my days are numbered,
My nerves are red and raw
For every now and then
I find a scratching at my door.

3. The Carrot Concerto

When Sir Simon rang me I felt quite rattled.
He said, "A concerto has been discovered
In a potting shed in Tooting Bec."
An obscure composer called Watt the Hek,
Had written it there and left it to rot,
For symphony band and solo carrot.
From this solitary shed,
He laboured intent,
Dug his vegetable bed,
For to him it a-lot-meant,
And planting the seeds,
For the music he seeks,
'Til his artichoke heart,
Sprang a bunch of leaks,
And he died for his art,
In a matter of weeks,
But his parting wish,
As he ended life's battle,
Was a world premiere,
With Sir Simon Rattle,
Who gave me a call,
For who else would dare to
Fill Symphony Hall,
With The Carrot Concerto.
With molto risotto!
Allegro tomato!
Andante potato!
Presto con marrow!
And dolce rhubarbo...
I played out my hearto,
My carrot was shattered,
I spat out the fragments,
Who knows where they landed.

But Sir Simon stood still, his emotions bare,
With carroty bits in his curly hair.
And everyone there will for ever recall,
That Carrot Concerto at Symphony Hall.

*The London Vegetable Orchestra at the Soho Theatre
performing in 'The Horne Section'*

4. The Food of Love

She said that she loved me,
I thought, what a thrill,
I'll open her heart with a tasty mixed grill,
Of sirloin and rump but she said that my food,
Was poison to her vegetarian mood,
And plying my suit I'd be wasting my time,
By taking my usual carnivorous line,
And cooking her gammon, or cutlets or chops,
While she was out browsing in greengrocers shops,
So I fettled my gherkins and gave her a squeeze,
And murmured, I love you, my sweet calabrese,
You're the beans in my pod, you're my sugar snap peas,
You're my pumpkin, my parsnip, my plump aubergine,
My spinach, my beetroot, my tasty spring greens,
And touching a leek to her cherry red lips,
And using my rocket to tickle her turnips,
I said that I wanted to get close and personal
I'd fondle her melons, she'd mangle my wurzle,
And soon I had seeded her vegetable plot,
And she'd screamed, oh my onions,
I said, that'shallot,
And we settled in bliss with our artichoke hearts,
As entwined as sweet peas, until blight do us part.
From a dream full of truckles of baby sweet corn,
Full of veggie intentions I rose with the dawn, and ran
to the garden, our own dew-drenched plot,
To find it dug over,
She'd purloined the lot, save
A handful of peas and a solitary carrot.
Now winter's winds freeze my green-fingered romance,
And I'm stood all alone like a man in a trance,
While my stir fried mung beans trip the fire alarm,
'Cos she's left for a man with an organic farm.

I take no further pleasure in burgers or steaks,
Or liver and bacon,
Because my heart aches.
My allotment is empty, of love I'm bereft,
A solitary carrot is all I have left.

5. Number Thirteen

Whenever I feel like a luxury treat,
A really exotic plate to eat,
My local place can't be oversold,
The Chew Fat in the Bromyard Road.
So on Friday I thought a visit I'd pay
With a very good friend from Leominster way,
And we ordered our food from Shanghai and Penang
When in walked the man with the Black Country twang.
He was broad he was loud he was full of blags,
With a couple of blondes with designer bags,
Gold on each arm, and a ten-grand phone
That his fingers could never leave alone,
And his aftershave was a musky pong
That totally ruined my egg foo yung,
And every minute someone rang
That awful man with the Black Country twang.
And he told us all in a grating shout,
Of travelling the world and eating out
of monkeys' brains with a golden spoon,
And bears' paws that had been barbecued.
And he bawled for the waiter and yelled for the chef,
And he screamed at the barmaid,
But the menu he left
upside down on the table unseen,
And smirked as he said,
"I'll take number thirteen."
"I always have that one," he shouted at me
"Cos you never know what the food's going to be,
And it keeps these slitty-eyed chinks on their toes
And it's always different wherever I goes."
"Number thirteen?" the waiter repeated,
"Are you sure, sir? Number twelve is well rated,
And thirty-four is our signature dish,
With shark fin soup and sliced raw fish."
"Are you deaf!" he yelled in his Dudley roar,

"I said thirteen not thirty-four,
And I'll tell your boss you're a useless knob
Who's come very close to losing his job."
And I looked at the menu, and here's the twist,
Number thirteen just didn't exist,
But twelve to fourteen ran without a break,
From chicken chow mein
To swordfish steak.
"Well," said the waiter, "that's a dish so rare,
We need a week to really prepare,
But we always want to treat you right
So the food's on the house for you every night
And just to get you on your way
We'll start with a banquet this very day."
"That's more like it!" said the Black Country man,
And all week they kept to their promised plan
And fed him on duckling and fatty stuff,
'Til some days he nearly cried enough!
And his skin grew sleek, and his buttocks grew slack,
And they dressed him in silks and massaged his back,
While beautiful Chinese girls gave in
To his every decadent wish and whim.
Then the chef gave the waiter a knowing wink,
And he said to the man, "We really think
You should visit the kitchen after hours,
'Cos number thirteen is almost yours."
And the cymbals clashed and the waiters sang
In praise of the man with the Black Country twang.
And the kitchen doors opened and closed as well,
And a terrible, awful silence fell.
Number thirteen's on the menu now,
And the name of Chew Fat is a name to know.
It's a smooth and unctuous carnivore's treat,
The softest skin and the sweetest meat,
And the critic's praise to the rafters rang
For its hint of musk, and its Black Country tang

6. A Christmas Carrot

When you're standing in the garden,
In the chill December snows,
There's a deep humiliation,
With a carrot for a nose.
I can suffer coal for eyes,
And an apparent lack of toes,
But it's just a step too far
To use a carrot for my nose.
Now a nose that's rather prominent
In literature is best.
Cyrano de Bergerac
Was singularly blessed,
And even young Pinocchio,
Whose nose kept getting bigger,
Was a hero in the end,
Though a rather wooden figure.
A bloodhound's nose can seek and find,
A hedgehog's nose can forage.
But mine's a frozen vegetable,
That's long and bright and orange.
Not aquiline or retroussé,
Roman, snub or parrot,
Oh who would be a snowman
When your nose is just a carrot?
The sparrows come and perch on it,
And make all sorts of fun
Of my frozen snotty icicles,
That dribble in the sun.
And if it starts to fall,
I haven't got a hand to grab it,
So it ends up on the ground,
And being nibbled by a rabbit.
So when you build a snowman,
Remember he has pride,
And that chilly white exterior
Hides a beating heart inside.

He has dreams and he has feelings,
Tho' it hardly ever shows,
So for the sake of Christmas cheer,
Don't use a carrot for his nose...

IV Relationships

Couplegate

1. Commitment

Would I like to... Miss? You ask me as we walk and talk
together,
I'm not sure I... knowing that my hand is given to
another
But we could... she wouldn't know, I tell myself, I'm
good at lying,
So I touch her... and I kiss her, easy, I'm not really
trying.

One girl goes, another follows,
Moans and cries and says she loves me,
Yeah, I say, it's all her hormones,
love's an illness of the lonely

What did you mean by... dear oh dear, I recognise the
usual question,
When you said... now when was that, I really, really
can't recall,
And where were you... I eye the door and mentally
rehearse my exit,
We need to talk... I want some sex, without the chat,
against the wall.

Life is great, all beer and skittles,
Films and lads and YouTube porn,
Curry, beans and comfort vittals,
Belch and scratch and fart and yawn,

Do I miss you... Miss? Now Mrs Jackson with a double buggy,
Can't believe we... but we did, behind the club against the wall,
Nice to see you... though you've cut your hair and grown a size or seven,
Catch you sometime... down the boozer, what's your number?
Gimme a call.

Usual table at the Social,
Club for over sixties only,
Love's a blue and distant country.
Love's a memory for the lonely.

2. She Told Me

She told me, grabbed my arm,
Said sotto voce, he's a shit, said he
Didn't care if I looked elsewhere,
Then smashed the place, because...
I did.

He told me, in the bar, right out loud,
She's a whore, just like her mum before,
But when I wanted sex today, she said,
No way!
She told me, in my ear, no one could hear,
I love a man, could he love me? If I was free?
I didn't know, I told her so,
Why question me?

He told me, I want out, without a doubt,
But when I said his girl was cute, he said,
I'll kill you, stay away,
I said OK.

She asked, what did he say?
I said, no way could I betray,
The confidence I heard,
He asked as well,
I said I wouldn't tell.
I didn't say a word.
But now my ears are burning,
Should I say they're both in error?
In my head two tales of sadness,
Can I bring them back together?
Don't think so.
Although I know,
They love,
Each other,
So.

3. A Class Act

I'm an ardent fan of duplicity,
A double-dealing ace.
I can lie with surprising facility,
And a genuine smile on my face.
I can spin you a web of deception,
With no kernel of truth at its heart,
And know by your friendly reception,
That I've mastered my shadowy art.
But then came the day that I dreaded,
When I wanted to tell you the truth.
And I struggled and stammered and blustered,
Like a lovesick and red-faced youth,
You looked with an air of suspicion,
And said "What are you trying to say?
I really suspect that you're lying!"
And you slapped me and walked away.
So the moral of my little story,
which I tell to you as a friend,
unless you want to be lonely,
Lie to the bitter end.

4. Loss

Something, somewhere is burning.
Something, somewhere is alight.
Through an air full of rain,
I smell smoke.
Someone, somewhere is hurting,
Someone, somewhere cries,
In an air full of rain,
I taste tears.
Somewhere, over there the sun is shining.
Somewhere, over there the earth is warm.
Over here I smell smoke, hear the rain, taste the tears.
I want to be over there with you in the sun.
In your gentle arms.
Why are my feet so heavy?
Why can't I see through the smoke?
Why does the rain taste like tears?
Why don't I know where to go?
Why won't you call my name?

5. Scent

The smells that take me back,
Back as far as I can go.
My grandma cooking bacon,
On her new electric stove,
While I hid under the table,
Waiting.
The hay barn where we slept,
While the country froze outside,
In a dusty darkness deep, we planned tomorrow's trips,
To the caves beneath the hill,
Together.
And the honeysuckled porch,
Where I kissed my red-haired girl.
How each flower I smell today,
Brings her back to me again,
And the door we leaned against,
Excited.
And now cycling through the dusky
Silence of a summer night.
Cold air in the valleys,
Fading azure light.
Passing through the farmyard.
The cows are in the barn
Honeysuckle beckons,
bonfires dying down.
Supper through the window,
Drifts into the lane,
Then riding up the hill
Where the warm day's air remains.
But the smell that I most treasure,
The one I must repeat,
That rises up to meet me
When I lift aside the sheet.
The one that strokes my senses
Like a soft and sensuous glove.
Slips into my heart and soul,
The dark, sweet scent of love.

6. Girlfriend

A red cloud trickled through the lager,
And a tooth rested on the glass's floor.
Pride kept her on her feet.
So he'd belted her in front of everyone,
Walked into the shocked crowd,
Then ran away.
"She must deserve it," they said.
Someone else said, "Shame."
The lager took a pinkish glow,
That picked up the UV,
And the tooth sat in a pale red
haze.
"She might have had AIDS," they said,
And no one would clear it away.
She walked from the bar,
And jumped from the bridge.
"Pride drove her," they said.
No one touched her,
"She might have had AIDS," they said.
"A shame," they said.
And drifted away.

The Sue Thompson challenge: to use the words red and lager in a poem.

7. Goodbye

Click, delete, one by one,
No photos to burn, crumpling to silvery ghosts,
Just click, delete, a file, a folder,
The holiday snap, the night in the pub,
The Facebook download,
Click, delete,
The favourite one, the rude one,
The intimate one,
The last one.

Cursor hovers.
Click, delete,
And empty the recycle bin,
Click,
Delete,
Goodbye.

The next poem comes with a health warning

'IT MAY OFFEND'

To maintain composure, please skip the next two pages...

8. On Seeing A Statue Of A Hermaphrodite In The Prado Museum In Madrid

When Hermes met with Aphrodite's charm,
The child, Hermaphroditus was their son,
Whose looks so captivated Salmacis,
She swore eternal love, eternal bliss,
And entwined the tender child in raping arms,
Creating a chimera, lithe and quick,
A pretty boy with boobies and a prick.

Now feminism's come and left its trace,
A well deserved kick for all mankind,
But scratch the surface of the female race,
And lift its edges, well, what do we find?

A small but strident retinue of women
A slighted, bitter, pierced and tattooed crowd,
With spiky hair and armoured double buggies,
With attitude and voices twice as loud,
As high-speed rail, tell us we're a mistake,
An aberration, God's only, greatest blunder,
A paedophile, a one eyed trouser snake,
Yet still an irritating source of wonder, so

They show their breasts, they smile, they spread their legs,
They take our seed to fertilise their eggs,
Then say, "Piss off, you're just a waste of space,
And, if I have your man-child, I'll make sure
That he's brought up to think just like a girl.
A perfectly hermaphroditic child,
A mind with thoughts so positive and pink,
He'll never push a woman to the brink."
With not a man in sight to teach him fighting, rough and tumble,
Or to take apart an engine on a pristine kitchen table,

Or take the risks a man will need to keep his family
stable.

A constant stream of criticism, sarcasm and wit,
Incessantly reminds us that we're just a piece of shit,
And erodes our self respect with all the venom you can
spit,
And leaves us wondering why we ever tried to be
polite,
And took you out and gave you things, and said it was
alright
To use our credit cards for rubbish just because you
felt uptight.

Yes, we were all just not quite good enough to entertain
your favours,
But when we're old and glaring at each other 'cross the
street,
And only turn our heads to stare at firmer breasts than
yours,
Remember how you thought that we could make your
life complete, but...

Remember how you sent us all a-packing one by one,
Remember how you trashed our feelings, said "Look
what you've done!
Oh I'd rather eat my toenails than give you the time of
day",
And gaze sadly at our coffins when we quietly pass
away.

*Dedicated to all the rejected fathers of this world, especially my
friend Steve, who pursued the mother of his daughter for many
years through the courts, before finally getting limited access.*

9. The Point Of Change

I see my children, image harried teens, whose parents,
simply tolerated, sadly tend the few brief times,
When they might feel they matter still.
And I think back towards another age.
At ten without a care you ruled
Your primary school with just a hint
Of fear at what the following year would bring.
And I think back to years of toddling bliss,
When hugs and kisses shared without a thought
Of who was watching on the street,
As stature, intellect and nature grew.
And I think back to baby on the breast,
That gave no thought what we could see or smell,
When filling nappies, wetting shoulders with a sweet
half-finished milky cheese
So startled when that lusty infant cry,
Welcomed the first taste of air,
The feel of sunlight, smell of doctor's hands.
And I think back to many months before,
And the moment you were made.
One of passion, or possession,
Romance or indifference,
Real intent, or just an idle moment in a marital bed?
Either way the change was made.
Cells that alone were powerless were joined as one
And blessed with power to grow.
To be the best among the best.
The limbs that grew, the eyes tight shut,
But other senses taking in
The hum of life, vibrations of the fluids moving in the
mother's heart,
The noise of traffic, morning music, evening news,
night time snoring,
Toilets flushing, showers running,
Cats that sat and purred above your head.
Arguments and words of love

Who knows what formed inside that growing mind?
Ideas of what the world would bring.
And all the strength you needed
For that one tremendous passage,
Pushed by muscles out of thought's control.
The stretching, skull-defining,
Agonising voyage through to our world.
To deliver, to deliver, to deliver.
That most momentous point of change in your young
life.
These points of change stand out for me.
These points of change you didn't see.
These points of change that made you be.
And yet there is another time of change,
Defined by doctors, writ in law,
Socially accepted, rich and poor,
Accept its judgement bleak,
And I would like to ask,
What is the key?
Where is that point of change and why?
That turns this growing child
Into a wonderful, anticipated,
Loved, protected, celebrated,
Spinster-softening, family-feted
member of our human race?
From a thing, whose little life,
At our convenience, or our lifestyle choice,
Can, without recrimination, repercussion, prosecution,
Or dissenting voice.
Be terminated.

V. The Environment
Where Was God?

One fine day 13.7 billion years ago,
Before the first stars began to glow,
A deity came up with a mighty plan,
"I'll make myself a universe, I'll make myself a man."

Now at the top of our evolutionary path,
On our beautiful blue planet, was he having a laugh?
'Cos scientists now rule the earth with all their bright ideas,
And give us bioengineered genetically modified cotton to wipe away our tears.

And we say...

Where was God - when the universe exploded?
Where was God - when our world began to spin?
Where was God - when we buggered up the planet?
'Cos we really need him now to come and sort the mess we're in!

Is he on his lunch break? - Is he having tea?
Does he even spare a thought for little you or me?
Is he listening to the cricket? Is he basking in the sun?
Well have no fear, 'cos science is here, and we're all having fun!!

Where was God - when we gave you nitroglycerine?
Where was God - when we handed you the bomb?
Where was God - when we blew up Hiroshima?
Enola Gay said bombs away and blew them all to kingdom come!

We've given you plutonium, uranium and strontium,
All packaged very nicely in a ghastly steaming brew,
We haven't got the faintest what we really want to do

with it,
So tell your great-grandchildren that we'll leave it all to
you.

We've taken your genetic code and turned it inside out,
And added little bits and bobs to make you thin or
stout,
If you want a blue-eyed baby you can have one for a
song,
And we'll give you one for spares as well when things
start going wrong.

We gave you a Mercedes and we told you what to do,
Just take our precious oil and turn it into CO_2,
At a hundred miles an hour in a ghastly gleaming roar,
And when the Arctic ice is gone we'll go and drill for
more.

There's a scientist with a test tube and a brown genetic
stew,
Making babies that are simply half a rabbit and half
you,
And we'll feed a generation growing up to super-size,
With a chicken that grows ready-cooked with
mayonnaise and fries.
Designer drugs will blow your mind in 50 different
ways,
and the secret chip beneath your skin will track you all
your days,
We know exactly what you eat and when you piss and
pooh,
And we'll process it discreetly and we'll feed it back to
you!

The mobile phone will fry your brain, the internet will
fuck it,
So take our new technology and tell us where to chuck

it,
Shout that digital society is rotten to the core,
But we won't fret, I'll place a bet, you'll soon be back
for more. Singing!!

Where was God - when we gassed the Jews in Buchenwald?
Where was God - when we napalmed Vietnam?
Where was God - playing snooker with the universe,
While we were dropping landmines in the name of Uncle Sam?!

We're really very happy in our air-conditioned dome,
'Cos we've geo-engineered the Earth and fried your
happy home,
And while you're gently stewing in a sulphurous
burning hell,
We'll fly away to Mars and make a mess of that as well!

Where was God - when the universe exploded?
Where was God - when our world began to spin?
Where was God - when we buggered up the planet?
'Cos we really need him now to come and sort the mess we're in!

Singing... Where was God!!!!

VI. A Poetical Self-Reflection

I Got Hugged By A Poet With Dreadlocks

And I wanted to hug him back,
But when I encounter dreadlocks
I'm not sure how to react.
Do you go round the front
Between neck and hair?
Do you go round the back,
If your hands can meet there?
Or brace yourself with strength unmatched,
And burrow within the tangled thatch,
Not knowing if, or even when
Your hands will ever escape again!
And if you do, then you'd better take care,
Deep inside,
In the poet's hair.
In the limerick the man of Liskeard,
Said it is just as I feared.
An owl and a hen,
Two larks and a wren,
Have all made their nests in my beard.
But dreads of a twentieth century kind
Must carry a more contemporary find.
A mobile phone, a packet of ten,
A credit card, or a ballpoint pen.
Or I may discover
His stash of weed,
Or a single Viagra,
For sexual need.
But I really hope I might find an elf
That takes my hand,
And draws me in to the poet's self,
Where his muse resides in a hut of hair,
With meaningful words stuck everywhere.
No fridge so Velcro does the task,

And now and then the poet asks for his latest work,
and his muse obliges.
So the question that occupies my head is
Can I write poems without the dreads?
Or would a hairpiece work instead?
Or must I twiddle my thumbs again,
Till my hair is as thick as a unicorn's mane,
And I have my own muse, my resident elf,
And he takes my words from his hairy shelf,
Like nothing I've written before myself.
A right-on, streetwise, rapid fire, up-to-date, cool
kid, stream of consciousness...
Or should I have a short back and sides and stick to
iambic pentameter...
Discuss.